contents

vegetarian asian

THE ESSENTIAL KITCHEN

INTRODUCTION TO vegetarian asian

The world of vegetarian Asian food is incredibly diverse and full of delicious choices. The majority of people living in South East Asia—China, Indonesia, Japan, Malaysia, the Philippines, Thailand, Laos, Burma, Sri Lanka, Vietnam, Taiwan and Korea—are vegetarian through choice, custom and agricultural circumstances. Because animal products are so resource intensive to produce in comparison to vegetables and grains, they are either reserved for special occasions, eaten in very small quantities, or not eaten at all. So by default millions of people have developed an unlimited variety of vegetarian recipes. This is in stark contrast to countries that can afford to eat animal products regularly and where a main meal may be considered incomplete if it does not contain meat, fish or poultry. But today, the fast, easy and healthy option of vegetarian Asian food is increasing in popularity throughout the world.

There are three basic categories of being vegetarian. Vegans avoid all products of animal origin regardless of whether or not an animal died to provide it. This includes meat, poultry and fish as well as dairy, honey, eggs, gelatin, and even wines filtered with egg whites.

Lacto-vegetarians eat dairy products such as milk, yogurt and cheese that has been made without rennet, a curdling agent originally taken from the stomach lining of cows. Ovo-lacto vegetarians eat dairy and eggs. There are also categories of semi-vegetarians. Pesco-vegetarians eat fish and seafood but not poultry or red meat; pollo-vegetarians eat chicken but not fish, seafood or meat. In many instances being vegetarian is a highly respected decision made in order to pursue a spiritual life.

To some inhabitants of India who are vegetarian for religious reasons, seafood and fish are described as "fruit of the sea" and are therefore eaten. Macrobiotics refers to the primarily vegetarian dietary system developed as a part of Zen Buddhism to prolong life.

There are many compelling reasons for choosing to eat more vegetarian food—or to go completely vegetarian—including health issues, environmental concerns about proper resource management, agribusiness practices, the treatment of animals destined for consumption, the safety of our food supply and the fact that a vegetarian diet is less expensive. There is absolutely no reason to assume that restrictive eating practices, righteousness or eating boring food have anything to do with vegetarian dining. For millions of people the vegetarian choice is both delicious and diverse.

Vegetarian Asian food is based on fresh vegetables and fruits combined with grains, seeds and legumes. Soybeans are vegetarian Asia's most important source of non-animal protein. The amazing array of food products made from soybeans includes tofu, tempeh, beancurd skins, soy milk, textured vegetable protein (TVP), soy sauce, miso, bean sauces, sprouts, oil, soy cheese and the beans themselves. In China soybeans are known as the "meat of the earth" and tofu is called "meat without a bone." On its own, tofu has little flavor, so generations of cooks have devised ways with tofu to add flavor, including techniques that look and taste exactly like any part of fish, meat or poultry.

The other most prevalent ingredient is undoubtedly rice, which has a place at many meals in one form or another. The two main categories are long-grain, including basmati and jasmine, and medium- or short-grain varieties, which may also be called glutinous or sticky rice because the grains cling together when cooked instead of staying separate. Rice preferences vary from country to country: for some separate fluffy grains are preferred while others choose a sticky result that is easy to eat with chopsticks.

One of the many reasons why vegetarian Asian food is healthy is the diversity of dishes eaten at once. All diets should ideally include as much variety as possible and this is especially so for non-meat eaters who need to get plenty of nutrients from many different sources. Combining different vegetable and grain dishes with legumes is an excellent way to achieve this variety. A perfect example of this is the Chinese tradition of yum cha, meaning "drink tea." Many different dishes are eaten and copious amounts of tea consumed around a large family table either at home or at a restaurant, especially at the weekend. The dishes are varied and some are quite rich, so the tea is an important digestive aid.

Meals in Asia are rarely divided into breakfast, lunch and dinner. In Bali, for example, the day's cooking is done in the morning and the prepared food is left out for the whole day. Members of the family simply eat what they want, when they want, without set meal times. Everyone may well be eating different foods at different times. Even when meal times are set, there will usually be many different dishes across all the food groups.

There are always plenty of condiments on the Asian table, such as fresh chopped chili pepper and soy, which allow each diner to perfectly season his or her dish according to taste and the various dishes chosen. As a result, the dishes themselves are sometimes quite neutral.

Fluctuations in food supplies and limited refrigeration across many parts of Asia have resulted in a rich tradition of preserving techniques including drying, salting and pickling. Food that has been treated in this way is often pungently flavored and adds a great deal to plainer vegetable and grain dishes. The flexibility of measurements—especially with seasonings where there are always a lot of condiments served on the side—is another part of the recipe equation. Recipes vary according to the ingredients available and the condiments served, as well as the tastes and disposition of the cook. For this reason measurements in this book should be used as a guideline and not as gospel. Always taste a prepared dish and think about the context in which it will be served to make sure the seasoning is correct for the situation. When seasoning, it is useful to bear in mind that many Asian dishes are not meant to be strongly flavored. The Chinese breakfast soup, congee, should taste primarily of bland watery rice, and properly made Japanese dashi stock should also be quite neutral. In some instances this is because the texture of the food is valued more highly than its flavor. Other dishes are emphatically the opposite—usually because of the addition of chili pepper, which is surely one of Asia's most loved and hottest ingredients. Another aesthetic consideration is appearance. Vegetables and fruits in both homes and restaurants are often exquisitely carved and cut and there is great emphasis on such details of presentation.

A rule of thumb when trying to work out what to drink with Asian food is to consider the ingredients being served. Most Asian food is grain based and grain-based spirits, such as rice wine (sake) and whisky, are appropriate. Other spirits are made from sugars and fruits. Barley-based beer is ideal and most Asian countries have favorites that are exported, including the dry Japanese Asahi or Kirin, malty Indonesian Bintang, Thailand's lager Singha and China's Tsingtao.

Wine purists might say it is impossible to match a single wine across the wide variety of dishes eaten at once, but there are some general guidelines. Mild vegetarian food is often ideal with soft red wines from Argentina, Chile and South Africa. Not-too-spicy salads serve well with many New World white wines. Spicier and hotter dishes are good with light Italian white wines such as Soave and the sweetness of Alsatian wines such as Gewürztraminer.

In addition to alcoholic beverages, Asian food pairs well with many non-alcoholic drinks. There is a preoccupation bordering on obsession with tea, including black (fermented), green (unfermented), oolong (semi-fermented) and flower-scented black tea. Flavored teas, such as fresh ginger, are also popular. Jasmine is a popular example served with yum cha in China, while in Japan the preference is for green tea where its preparation is elevated to an art form in the tea ceremony. Tea contains plenty of antioxidants, which help mop up the damage done by free radicals, but more importantly it has a vital place in the cultural life of people who enjoy its flavors and rich traditions.

There is an extraordinary range of other non-alcoholic drinks commonly served at Asian meals. These include chilled coconut juice sipped straight from young coconuts with a straw; avocado blended with ice and condensed milk into a kind of thick shake; lime water; a variety of coconut milk and fruit drinks; chilled brewed coffee and tea sweetened and tossed together over ice with sago; salty sour milk or buttermilk; sweetened and flavored soy drinks; and fruit nectars. Some of these drinks are also enjoyed instead of a meal, as a sweet or as a cooling treat at any time of day.

In this book you'll find fast one-course meals as well as all the essential elements required for an Asian-inspired banquet. Explanations of common ingredients and cooking methods make it simple for novice cooks to experiment with new flavors, while experienced cooks will enjoy the diversity of vegetarian Asian cooking. The coded index makes it easy to choose recipes that are suitable for either vegans or ovo-lacto vegetarians, and both pesco- and pollo-vegetarians will find plenty of vegetable-based recipes to add to. Recipes are easy to prepare and based on simple cooking techniques with an emphasis on the freshness and flavor of authentic dishes and exciting variations.

ingredients

1.

2.

3.

4.

5.

6.

7.

8.

9.

10.

11.

12.

1. Bamboo shoots: It's best to choose pre-cooked vacuum-packed or canned shoots because not all types of bamboo are edible and even those that are require cooking to remove their toxicity. Commercial shoots are ready to slice and add to soups, stir-fries and curries.

2. Black vinegar: This essential flavor of Beijing food can be made from a variety of grains. The best, Chinkiang, is made from malt and glutinous rice. It has a complex flavor with no accurate substitute. Try it on noodle and vegetable dishes.

3. Chinese napa cabbage (wong nga bak): This long, delicately flavored cabbage is one of Asia's most common ingredients. It turns up raw in salads, steamed, stir-fried, pickled or braised. Bugs love it, too, so it needs to be well washed before cooking.

4. Choy sum (flowering cabbage): Choy sum is a tender leaf with pretty yellow flowers, all of which is edible. It is popular in Malaysia, China and Japan and requires a good rinse before steaming, stir-frying or simmering in broths.

5. Enoki: These delicate Japanese mushroom bundles have a small cap on a long tender stalk. They bring beauty, tenderness and a delicious yeasty lemon flavor that is valued in raw salads, stir-fries and clear soups.

6. Fried (French) shallots: These are widely available already prepared. Commercial shallots are finely sliced, deep-fried until crisp and golden, then stored in airtight jars. Fried shallots are also easy to prepare at home. To make, gently stir-fry in hot oil until golden and crisp. They are often scattered across finished dishes as a condiment.

7. Glutinous (sticky) rice – black, white or purple: Short-grain sticky rice is sticky after cooking because of its high starch content. It is the rice used in sushi. Many Asian rice desserts use this variety, and it is also a popular dim sum dish when wrapped in lotus leaves and steamed. It can take longer than other rice varieties to cook so soaking in water overnight is often recommended.

8. Hokkien noodles: Thick, fresh hokkien noodles are oiled to prevent them sticking and sold in vacuum packs from the refrigerator section. They add bulk and flavor to many noodle dishes, especially those from Malaysia and China.

9. Konbu (kelp): Seaweed or sea vegetables are a valuable source of nutrients, especially minerals, in a typical Asian diet. Konbu is usually sold dried in the west, although in Japan it is available fresh. Essential for Japanese dashi stock (see page 18 for recipe), konbu also improves the digestibility of dried beans. Also known as kombu.

10. Lotus root: This vegetable is prized for its sweetness and pretty appearance when sliced. Peel fresh lotus and slice thinly for deep-frying as chips, steaming as a vegetable or braising with other vegetables. It discolors quickly when cut, so work fast or rub the slices with lemon to prevent browning.

11. Palm sugar: Made from the sap of palm trees, this sugar is sweet, malty and rich. It is sold in syrup form or grated from solid blocks. The darker the color, the more intense the flavor. Brown sugar tastes similar, and can be substituted, but the flavor of palm sugar is superior.

12. Pandan (screwpine) leaf: Not all pandan varieties are edible, but those that are enjoy great popularity in Asian dishes. Their sweet and musky scent is a common ingredient in soups, rice, curries and desserts. Use the fresh or frozen leaf to infuse flavor in the dish then remove it before serving.

13.

14.

15.

16.

17.

18.

19.

20.

21.

22.

23.

24.

13. Pea shoots: Sold in large bags at Asian grocers, pea shoots are a common ingredient in salads or as a simple steamed green side dish. Tossed with vegetarian oyster sauce and ginger, or black vinegar and sesame oil, they are delicious and quick to prepare. Substitute bean shoots if pea shoots are unavailable.

14. Rice sheet noodles: These solid white cakes of fresh noodle need to be sliced then gently teased apart in boiling water before stir-frying or adding to soups. Buy them fresh and use at once as they lose their texture quickly.

15. Shiitake mushrooms: Shiitake are available fresh or dried. They are a prized antioxidant and frequently recommended to increase longevity. Sliced and added to dishes with vegetables or other mushrooms, they impart a rich flavor and firm texture. Soak dried shiitake in hot water for half an hour before using.

16. Shiso (perilla or beefsteak leaf): Shiso is related to mint and basil, but tastes nothing like either of them. It is used as a herb, but is not usually available fresh. More typically the red leaves are used to color and flavor umeboshi plums and gari (pink pickled ginger).

17. Starch balls: Many drinks in Asian countries include clear balls or beads of starch that don't taste of anything much, but they lend a much loved gelatinous texture to the drink. Sago, tapioca and potato flour balls are just some of the possibilities. They are quite addictive.

18. Szechuan pepper: Szechuan pepper is not related to black pepper and it has a tingly citrus rather than hot taste. It is an essential ingredient in many Chinese dishes. Use it roasted and ground with salt to sprinkle on vegetable and legume snacks or use in place of black pepper and salt over cooked foods.

19. Tamarind: This fruit comes from a tropical tree belonging to the pea family. Its sour, citrus flavor is essential to many Asian dishes. The coarse and sticky flesh can be difficult to separate from the seeds so a prepared paste is preferable. It keeps well in the refrigerator.

20. Tempeh: This fermented soybean cake originated in Indonesia and is now one of the vegetarian world's most valuable sources of protein and vitamin B12. It is used in place of meat and can be fried, steamed, boiled or broiled (grilled). It is has a firmer texture than tofu.

21. Tofu (bean curd) puffs: Pre-fried tofu pieces are quite light and porous, which makes them ideal for adding to any flavorsome dish with lots of liquid such as laksa, curries and soups.

22. Turmeric: This rhizome belonging to the ginger family is valued throughout South East Asia for the vibrant yellow color and particular flavor it imparts to food. It is available fresh or dried and ground. In Thailand, the young shoots are served as a vegetable.

23. Umeboshi plums: These are actually pickled apricots, not plums, used whole or as a puree in traditional Japanese food. The pickling liquid is available as a vinegar and has the same uses as other vinegars. Umeboshi has a deliciously salty, sour and fruity flavor. Apple cider vinegar is a good substitute.

24. Yard long (snake/long) beans: This fresh bean is also the source of dried black-eye beans. In its fresh form it should be firm and crisp. Once the ends are trimmed, the long strips are ready to be used in all the same ways as other fresh green beans.

equipment

1.

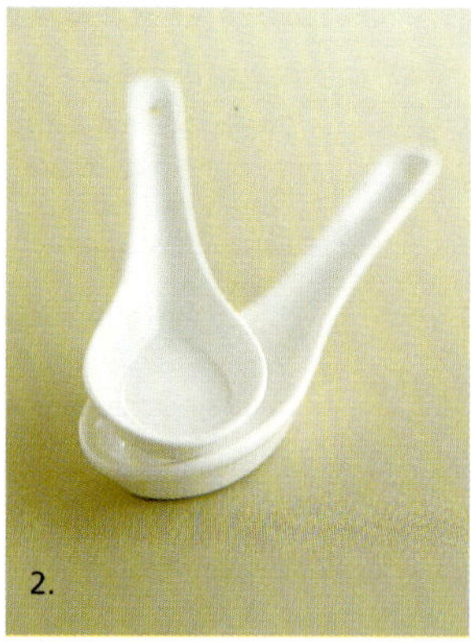

2.

3.

4.

5.

6.

7.

8.

9.

10.

11.

12.

1. Chinese chopper: Used for preparing vegetables, crushing garlic and spreading har gau dough into rounds.

2. Chinese porcelain spoons: Used for serving sauces and for eating some soups. Also handy to have for frequent taste testing.

3. Frying pan: Use a quality heavy-based version as a wok alternative. A non-stick frying pan is ideal for paper-thin omelettes.

4. Grater: Essential hand tool for finely grating ginger, hard vegetables and palm sugar.

5. Japanese vegetable slicer: Ideal tool for cutting wafer-thin raw vegetables for salads and soup garnishes as well as ginger for pickling.

6. Medium, heavy-based pot: Necessary for making curries, soups and noodles. Thin-based pots may allow garlic and spice pastes to scorch rather than color and rice will stick easily.

7. Mortar and pestle (or Japanese suribachi): Essential for pounding dry spice mixes and curry pastes, and to crush rice for mochi (page 47).

8. Steamer: Made from aluminium or traditional bamboo, and used for steaming an infinite array of foods. Steaming is a very common Asian cooking technique.

9. Sushi mat: Essential for making sushi rolls, this specialized rolling mat can be used to squeeze excess liquid from vegetables such as cabbage before using them in salads.

10. Tongs and chopsticks: A good pair of tongs is like an extension of your hands great for handling the hot stuff. Use chopsticks to gently separate noodles and for serving.

11. Wok: The traditional pan used for fast stir-fries and for deep-frying small quantities of food. The narrow base requires just a little oil to be deep enough for frying.

12. Wooden spoons: Necessary for a reassuring stir and to check that thick sauces are not sticking to the base of the pot.

STEP-BY-STEP

perfect rice

White rice

Plain steamed white rice is the most popular accompaniment to Asian food. Other types of rice, such as black, glutinous (sticky) or brown, require different amounts of water and cooking time.

Step 1

If the rice was purchased from a bulk supply, rinse well and check for debris.

For every 1 cup (7 oz / 220 g) rice, measure 2 cups (16 fl oz / 500 ml) water and 1 teaspoon salt (optional).

Put the rice, water and salt in a heavy-based pot with a capacity of at least 62 fl oz (2 L). Place the pot uncovered over a high heat and bring to a boil.

Step 2

At boiling, stir the rice once only to ensure no grains stick to the base of the pot. Reduce the heat to its lowest level.

Step 3

Cover the pot with a tight-fitting lid and cook until all the water is absorbed, about 15 minutes.

Remove the pot from the heat and set aside for 5–10 minutes. The grains of rice will continue to expand.

Step 4

Using a fork, fluff the grains of rice. Serve immediately. One cup (7 oz / 220 g) raw rice makes about 3 cups (15 oz / 450 g) cooked rice.

Serves 4

Brown rice

2 cups (13 oz / 400 g) uncooked short grain brown rice
$2^3/_4$–3 cups water (22–24 fl oz / 685–750 ml), depending on texture preference
$^1/_4$ teaspoon salt

Although short-grain brown rice does not cling as easily as short- grain white rice, its nutty flavor and chewier texture make an interesting alternative.

Rinse brown rice once and cook until most liquid is absorbed, about 30–35 minutes. Remove from heat and stand, covered, 10–15 minutes longer. The absorption method in a saucepan or microwave also works well with brown rice.

wrapping

While foods beautifully wrapped in banana leaves at Asian market stalls look very special, this simple tradition is born of practicality. Unlike modern commercial packaging, these takeaway materials are readily available, inexpensive and entirely biodegradable.

Step 1

Cut fresh banana leaves into roughly 8-inch (20-cm) squares.

Then cut further banana leaves into an equal number of strips, roughly 1/4 x 8 inch (6 mm x 20 cm). Pair each square with one strip.

Step 2

Steam the squares and strips until they are soft and pliable, about 5 minutes. Remove from the steamer and spread on a work surface.

Step 3

Place 1 cup (8 oz / 250 ml) of prepared food, such as rice and vegetables or tofu curry, in the center of each square.

Step 4

Gather up the edges, making sure the contents are completely enclosed. Tie firmly using the strip of leaf. Do not pull too hard or the leaf will tear.

Either steam immediately, allowing 15–20 minutes for the food to be hot, or refrigerate until ready to cook.

Variation

Make smaller parcels for bite-size servings. Also try using bread-fruit, dried bamboo, taro or lotus leaves. Tie these smaller leaves with strips of pandan or string.

Ginger sesame dressing

$^{1}/_{4}$ cup (2 fl oz / 60 ml) umeboshi or apple cider vinegar
2 tablespoons peeled and finely grated ginger
$^{1}/_{2}$ cup (4 fl oz / 125 ml) light sesame oil

Blend ingredients until smooth and creamy. Use as a dressing for raw coleslaw vegetables, such as finely sliced red or green cabbage, grated carrot and chopped parsley, or over steamed greens or corn on the cob. Store in refrigerator for up to 1 week.

Makes ¼ cup (6 fl oz / 180 ml)

Fresh pickled ginger

1 cup (4 oz / 120 g) fresh, peeled and paper-thin sliced ginger
$^{1}/_{2}$ teaspoon fine salt
2 tablespoons superfine (caster) sugar
$^{1}/_{4}$ teaspoon shiso or perilla leaf (optional)
$^{1}/_{4}$ cup (2 fl oz / 60 ml) white vinegar

Toss the ginger with salt, cover and set aside overnight. Drain and remove excess moisture with paper towel. Add the sugar and shiso leaf if using. Stir in the vinegar. Pack in a sterilized glass jar. Refrigerate for one week before using, giving the jar a shake each day. Pickled ginger is traditionally served with sushi and nori rolls. It is also good finely chopped and mixed through salads, especially if the salad contains boiled egg or potato. Store in refrigerator for up to 1 month.

Makes 1 cup (4 oz / 120 g)

Sesame salt | (gomasio)

1 cup (5 oz / 150 g) white sesame seeds
2 teaspoons sea salt

Variation

Instead of salt, dry roast 1 oz (30 g) seaweed and grind to a powder with the toasted sesame seeds.

Rinse the seeds. Drain and just cover with fresh water. Stir in the salt, cover and set aside overnight. Drain. Heat a non-stick frying pan over medium-high heat and add the seeds. Dry toast the seeds, stirring regularly so the seeds on the bottom do not stick, until the seeds are golden brown, finish popping and smell nutty, 8–12 minutes. Remove from the pan and spread out to cool. They should be quite dry. When cool, grind them gently using a mortar and pestle or suribachi (Japanese mortar and pestle) until the seeds are half crushed. Use as a seasoning. Store in a sealed jar for up to 2 weeks.

Makes 1 cup (5 oz / 150 g)

Szechuan pepper and salt mix

5 teaspoons whole Szechuan pepper
1 teaspoon sea salt

Heat a non-stick frying pan over medium-high heat. Add the pepper and gently roll it around the dry surface for about 3 minutes. Remove from the heat and tip the pepper onto a flat surface to cool. When cool, combine the pepper with the salt and grind to a fine consistency. Store in a sealed jar for up to 2 weeks. Use in place of salt and black pepper as a seasoning for vegetable dishes.

Makes 3 tablespoons

Fresh coconut cream

1 cup (3 oz / 90 g) freshly grated coconut
2 cups (16 fl oz / 500 ml) boiling water

Place the coconut and half the hot water in a blender. Leave for one minute, then blend until smooth, about 1 minute. Strain through a cheesecloth-lined strainer set over a medium-sized bowl. Press as much of the liquid as possible through the cloth and set the liquid aside. This liquid is thick coconut cream. Return the coconut pulp to the blender. Add the remaining water. Leave for 1 minute, then blend again until quite smooth, about 2 minutes. Press as much of the liquid as possible through a fresh piece of cheesecloth and strainer. This liquid is thin coconut cream. The thick and thin coconut creams may be kept separate or mixed together, depending on the recipe. Thick coconut cream has a richer flavor. Both will spoil quickly, so they should be prepared the day they are required and refrigerated until needed. Stores in refrigerator for 12 hours.

Makes 2 cups (16 fl oz / 500 ml)

Lemongrass, chili and soy dipping sauce

1 stalk lemongrass
¼ cup (2 fl oz / 60 ml) light or dark soy sauce
2 small red chili peppers, seeded and finely sliced

Cut off the thick base of the lemongrass stalk and remove the outer leaves. Keep the tough stalk and leaves for use in soups and curries. Bash the fleshy base then chop it finely. It will be a little fibrous. Mix the lemongrass with the soy sauce and chili. Store in a glass jar in the refrigerator. Especially good as a dipping sauce for wontons (see page 32) and dumplings (see page 29). Mix with 2 tablespoons vegetable oil and use as a dressing for steamed green vegetables. Store in refrigerator for up to 2 weeks.

Makes ¼ cup (2 fl oz / 60 ml)

Chili, black vinegar and sesame dressing

¼ cup (2 fl oz / 60 ml) Chinese black vinegar
2 small red chili peppers, seeded and finely sliced
1 tablespoon finely chopped scallions (shallots / spring onions)
¼ cup (2 fl oz / 60 ml) peanut oil
1 teaspoon dark sesame oil

Combine the vinegar, chili and scallions. Whisk in the peanut and sesame oils. Store in a glass jar in the refrigerator. Toss through noodle dishes, particularly thick Chinese wheat noodles, use as a salad dressing or as a sauce for steamed mixed vegetables. Store in refrigerator for up to 2 weeks.

Makes ½ cup (4 fl oz / 125 ml)

Basic chili sambal

- 3 small red chili peppers, seeded and finely sliced
- pinch salt
- $^1/_4$ teaspoon white vinegar
- 1 teaspoon peanut oil

Mix the chili peppers, salt and vinegar in a small blender or crush by hand in a mortar and pestle to form a smooth paste. Do not lean over the mix while blending because the volatile fumes from chili are a potent irritant. Scrape the paste into a small serving dish and cover with peanut oil. Serve as a condiment with steamed mixed vegetables and yum cha dishes (see pages 28-37). Store larger amounts in a glass jar in the refrigerator, protecting the surface from the air with peanut oil, for up to 2 weeks.

Makes 2 tablespoons

Red, yellow or black bean paste

- 1 cup (7 oz / 220 g) dried aduki (red), dried and split mung (yellow) or soy (black) beans
- $^3/_4$ cup (6 oz / 185 g) superfine (caster) sugar
- pinch salt

Note

The time required to cook beans until tender will vary depending on the bean variety and the age of the beans. The older and therefore drier the beans, the longer they will take to soften. Cut cooking time by two thirds if using a pressure cooker.

Check chosen bean variety carefully for stones and debris. Rinse thoroughly with plenty of water. Cover with fresh water and soak overnight. After soaking, drain well and cover with fresh water so that there is about 1 inch (2.5 cm) above the beans. Bring to a boil. Boil uncovered for 10 minutes. Reduce heat, half cover and simmer until tender and little of the water remains, about 45 minutes to 2 hours. Once the beans are tender, stir in the sugar and salt. Simmer until the water evaporates and the paste thickens, 10–15 minutes. Mash the beans with the back of a wooden spoon to the consistency of mashed potato. Cool. For a smoother finish, pass through a sieve or potato ricer. Use as a sweet filling in steamed buns or har gau pastry, eat on its own, or enjoy with a spoonful of thin or thick coconut milk in a sweet dessert soup or jelly, or in the Japanese way over green tea sorbet. Store in refrigerator for up to 1 week.

Makes 1½ cups (10 oz / 330 g)

Japanese plum and vegetable pickles

- 5 tablespoons ($2^1/_2$ oz / 75 g) umeboshi plum paste
- $3^1/_2$ cups (28 fl oz / 880 ml) water
- 1 cup (5 oz / 150 g) carrots, peeled and julienned into $^1/_4$ x 2 inch (6 mm x 5 cm) strips
- 1 cup (5 oz / 150 g) lotus root or celery, cut into $^1/_4$ inch (6 mm) slices
- 1 cup (4 oz / 125 g) small cauliflower florets
- 1 cup (4 oz / 125 g) red bell pepper, seeded and cut into strips

Mix the plum paste and water and set aside. Combine the prepared vegetables and pack firmly into a sterilized jar. Add the plum water and shake so the water disperses through the vegetables. Cover with cheesecloth and refrigerate for 4–6 days, giving the jar a shake each day. Seal the jar and refrigerate until needed. Serve as a snack or condiment with vegetables and grains. Stores in refrigerator for up to 2 weeks.

Makes 4 cups (1 lb / 500 g)

Ginger and spice broth

- 1 tablespoon vegetable oil
- 1 medium yellow onion, chopped
- 3 lemongrass stalks, bruised
- 4 cloves garlic, chopped
- 2 small red chili peppers, seeded and chopped
- 2 curry leaves
- 2 kaffir lime leaves, finely sliced
- 1-inch (2.5-cm) piece fresh galangal, peeled and chopped
- 2-inch (5-cm) piece fresh ginger, peeled and chopped
- 1 tablespoon grated palm sugar
- pinch salt
- 7 cups (56 fl oz / 1.75 L) clear vegetable stock
- 2 tablespoons lemon juice
- 2 tablespoons cilantro (coriander) leaves, chopped
- 1/2 lb (250 g) enoki or oyster (abalone) mushrooms
- 4 sprigs watercress

Warm the oil in a large pot over medium-high heat. Add the onion, lemongrass, garlic, chili, curry and kaffir lime leaves, galangal, ginger and sugar. Stir-fry until the aromas start to release, about 2 minutes. Add the salt, stock and lemon juice and bring to a boil. Simmer, uncovered, for 10 minutes. Strain, return the broth to a clean pot and discard the vegetables and spice. Return to a boil. Divide the cilantro, mushrooms and watercress equally between 4 bowls. Pour the broth over the vegetables. Serve immediately.

Serves 4

Variation

Use steamed choy sum or bok choy leaves instead of watercress.

Chinese noodle soup

Warm the oil in a wok over medium-high heat. Stir-fry the carrots, bamboo shoot tips and mushrooms for 3 minutes. Add the choy sum, scallions and bean sprouts and stir-fry for another minute. Stir in the sugar, salt, sherry and soy sauce. Meanwhile, cook the noodles in boiling water for 2 minutes. Drain, rinse in cold water and drain again. Add the cooked noodles to the simmering stock and return to a boil. Stir in the vegetables. Divide among individual soup bowls. Serve with extra soy sauce to taste.

Serves 4–6

1 tablespoon vegetable oil
1 medium carrot, peeled and sliced into flowers
4 oz (130 g) bamboo shoot tips, julienned
10 dried shiitake mushrooms, soaked in hot water for 30 minutes and drained
1/2 bunch (8 oz / 250 g) choy sum (flowering cabbage) leaves, roughly chopped
3 scallions (shallots / spring onions), trimmed and cut into 1 inch (2.5cm) pieces
1 cup (1 oz / 30 g) bean sprouts
1 teaspoon superfine (caster) sugar
1/2 teaspoon salt
1 tablespoon rice wine vinegar or sherry
2 tablespoons light soy sauce, plus extra for serving
10 oz (300 g) fresh flat egg noodles
8 cups (64 fl oz / 2 L) clear vegetable stock, simmering

Note

To curl scallions, slice the green part into very thin, long strips and plunge into ice water for 10 minutes. When they are in tight curls, drain and use as a garnish.

To make carrot flowers, cut carrots into slices 1/8 inch (3 mm) thick. Using a small, flower-shaped cookie (pastry) cutter, press the cutter into the carrots for the desired shapes.

Short soup

pieces of dried konbu (seaweed), about 6 inches (15 cm) square in total
8 dried shiitake mushrooms, soaked in hot water for 30 minutes and drained
8 cups (64 fl oz / 2 L) water
2 scallions (shallots / spring onions), trimmed and finely sliced on an angle

WONTONS
16 square wonton wrappers
1/2 batch Steamed garlic chive and shiitake dumplings filling (see page 29)

To make the wontons: Spread out the wonton wrappers and divide the filling between them, placing it neatly in the center of each square. Dampen the edges of each wrapper. Fold the wrapper over the filling to form a triangle. Gather the edges together firmly and squeeze them to secure. Steam on waxed paper in a steamer basket for 10 minutes.

To make the konbu dashi: Wipe the konbu with a damp cloth and place in a large pot with 4 of the mushrooms and the water. Bring to a boil, reduce the heat, and simmer, uncovered, for 20 minutes. Remove from the heat and discard the konbu and shiitake.

Transfer the wontons to individual soup bowls. Ladle the hot broth over the wontons. Scatter the top with scallions and the remaining shiitake.

Serves 4–5

Variation

Spice the broth, which is traditionally quite neutral in flavor, with the addition of ginger, lemongrass, kaffir lime and chili. Simply add a little of each after removing the konbu and shiitake, simmer for 10 minutes and strain before serving.

Corn, pumpkin, spinach and rice soup

Warm the oils in a large pot over medium-high heat. Add the onion and stir-fry until the onion begins to color, about 2 minutes. Add the ginger, corn kernels, pumpkin, rice and salt and stir-fry until the mix is coated with oil, about 1 minute. Add the water and bring to a boil. Reduce the heat and simmer, covered, until the vegetables and rice are tender and beginning to break up, about 50 minutes. Either leave the soup as it is, or blend to a puree. Reheat the spinach in a steamer. Mix the spinach with the salt and a drizzle of sesame oil. Divide the soup into individual bowls. Add the spinach in the center of each bowl. Serve with the sambal.

Serves 6–8

1 teaspoon sesame oil
2 tablespoons vegetable oil
1 medium yellow onion, chopped
1 piece fresh ginger, 2-inch (5-cm), peeled and finely chopped
6 ears of corn, kernels removed
2 cups (10 oz 300 g) peeled pumpkin, cut into chunks
1/4 cup (2 oz / 60 g) short or medium grain white rice
1/2 teaspoon salt
6 cups (48 fl oz / 1.5 L) water
1 cup (7 oz / 200 g) cooked and drained spinach
pinch salt
sesame oil, to taste
chili sambal, to taste (see page 15)

Thai hot and sour soup (tom yum)

1 tablespoon vegetable oil
1 medium yellow onion, chopped
3 lemongrass stalks, bruised
2 cloves garlic, chopped
3 small red chili peppers, 2 whole, 1 seeded and finely sliced
2 kaffir lime leaves, finely sliced
7 cups (56 fl oz / 1.75 L) clear vegetable stock, simmering
1 teaspoon superfine (caster) sugar
pinch salt
2 tablespoons lemon juice
1 tablespoon tamarind paste, soaked in $^1/_4$ cup (2 fl oz / 60 ml) water and strained
1 lb (500 g) canned straw mushrooms, drained and halved
4 scallions (shallots / spring onions), trimmed and finely chopped
2 tablespoons cilantro (coriander) leaves or Thai (holy) basil, chopped

Warm the oil in a large pot over medium-high heat. Add the onion and stir-fry until the onion begins to color, about 2 minutes. Add the lemongrass, garlic, 2 whole chilies, and kaffir lime leaves and fry for 1 minute. Add the vegetable stock, sugar and salt and simmer, uncovered, for 15 minutes. Strain the broth and transfer the liquid to a clean pot. Return to a boil and add the lemon juice, tamarind water and mushrooms. Divide among individual soup bowls. Sprinkle with a combination of scallions, seeded and sliced chili and cilantro or Thai basil.

Serves 4–6

Congee or rice water (Chinese breakfast soup)

Put the rice or mixed grains and water into a medium-large saucepan over high heat and bring to a boil. Stir the rice to make sure it does not stick to the base of the saucepan. Reduce the heat so the water is barely simmering and cover tightly so that the rice water does not bubble over the top. Simmer until the rice or the mixed grains split and are held in suspension in the water, about 90 minutes. Transfer the congee into individual bowls and offer small quantities of a selection of accompaniments.

Serves 6–8

1 cup (7 oz / 220 g) short-grain white rice or pre-mixed congee grains and legumes
6 cups (48 fl oz / 1.5 L) water

ACCOMPANIMENTS

1 teaspoon fried (French) shallots (see page 8)
1 tablespoon scallions (shallots / spring onions), finely sliced or curled
1 tablespoon fried peanuts
1 tablespoon dark sesame oil
2 small red chili peppers, seeded and finely sliced
1 tablespoon fermented black beans
1 tablespoon light soy sauce
1 tablespoon cilantro (coriander), chopped

Variations

Vary rice congee by adding different single ingredients—such as carrot, celery, fennel, ginger, leek, mustard, sesame seed or spinach—at the beginning of cooking. Instead of white rice, brown or sweet rice may also be used, as can other single grains such as spelt or millet.

Note

The nourishing properties of congee are said to increase with a longer cooking time of anywhere up to 6 hours. To do this, increase the water up to 10 cups (80 fl oz / 2.5 L), cook in a heavy-based saucepan so the rice will not stick, and simmer over very low heat.

To curl scallions, slice the green part into very thin, long strips and plunge into ice water for 10 minutes. When they are in tight curls, drain and use as a garnish.

Asian greens, peanut and bean thread noodle salad

- 3 oz (90 g) dried cellophane (bean thread) noodles
- 1 bunch (13 oz / 400 g) bok choy, trimmed and washed
- 1 bunch (16 oz / 500 g) choy sum, trimmed and washed
- 1/4 Chinese cabbage, washed
- 1 red (Spanish) onion, peeled and sliced into thin half moons
- 1/3 cup (2 oz / 50 g) peanuts, toasted and coarsely chopped
- 1 1/2 tablespoons white vinegar
- 3 tablespoons fresh lime juice
- 1 tablespoon tamarind paste
- 2 1/2 tablespoons superfine (caster) sugar
- 3 tablespoons peanut oil
- 1/4 cup (1/3 oz / 10 g) chopped Vietnamese or common mint
- 1/4 cup (1/3 oz / 10 g) chopped cilantro (coriander)

Soak the noodles in cold water until they start to soften, about 15 minutes. Drain and cut into roughly 4-inch (10-cm) lengths. Drop into a pot of boiling water and simmer until just tender, 2–5 minutes depending on the thickness of the noodles. Drain, rinse and drain again. Drain the noodles very well or the salad will be watery. Set aside. Cut the bok choy, choy sum and cabbage into roughly 1-inch (2.5-cm) squares, and the coarser stems into fine diagonal slices. Steam until just tender but still crisp, about 2 minutes. Rinse and drain. In a bowl, combine the noodles, steamed vegetables and remaining ingredients. Mix well, cover and chill for 30 minutes before serving.

Serves 4–6

Balinese cabbage and coconut salad

Blanch the cabbage, beans and beans sprouts separately—drop them into boiling salted water, return to the boil, drain and rinse under cold water. Squeeze out all excess moisture. Mix with the cooked spinach. Add the remaining ingredients and toss well. Serve immediately at room temperature. Accompany with glutinous (sticky) rice.

Serves 4–6

- 1 Chinese cabbage, cut into 1-inch (2.5-cm) squares
- 1 cup (7 oz / 220 g) yard long (snake) or green beans, cut into 1-inch (2.5-cm) lengths
- 1 cup (2 oz / 60 g) bean sprouts
- 1 cup (7 oz / 220 g) steamed and drained spinach
- 4 tablespoons fried (French) shallots (see page 8)
- 2 tablespoons vegetable oil
- 1 medium yellow bell pepper (capsicum), seeded and julienned
- 3 cloves garlic, minced
- 3 small red chilies, seeded and finely sliced
- 2 kaffir lime leaves, finely sliced
- 1/2 teaspoon superfine (caster) sugar
- 2 tablespoons lime or lemon juice
- 1/2 teaspoon salt
- pinch black pepper
- 1/2 cup (1 1/2 oz / 45 g) fresh grated or flaked coconut

Green papaya, cashew and bean salad

1 cup (7 oz / 220 g) yard long (snake) or green beans, cut into 2-inch (5-cm) lengths
1 cup (7 oz / 220 g) cooked and drained spinach
1 cup (7 oz / 220 g) green papaya, peeled and seeded, thinly sliced lengthwise
$^1/_2$ teaspoon salt
2 tablespoon grated palm sugar
$^1/_4$ cup (2 fl oz / 60 ml) mirin
2 tablespoons vegetable oil
$^1/_3$ cup (2 oz / 50 g) toasted and finely chopped cashew nuts
3 scallions (shallots / spring onions), finely sliced on an angle

Steam the beans until deep green but still crisp, about 2 minutes. Rinse under cold water and drain. Toss with the spinach and papaya. Add the salt, sugar, mirin and oil. Combine well. Serve strewn with cashew and scallions, on its own or paired with steamed rice.

Serves 4–6

Hot and sour salad

In a large bowl, combine the snow peas, snow pea shoots, bean sprouts, carrots and corn. Mix the remaining ingredients in a blender until smooth. Thoroughly mix the dressing through the vegetables and serve immediately.

Serves 4–6

2 cups (4 oz / 120 g) snow peas (mange tout), trimmed and steamed until tender
2 cups (1 oz / 30 g) pea shoots
1 cup (2 oz / 60g) bean sprouts
1 cup (4 oz / 125 g) carrots, julienned
1 cup (6 oz / 185 g) baby corn, steamed until tender and halved lengthwise
1 tablespoon umeboshi paste
pinch salt
$^1/_4$–$^1/_2$ teaspoon dried chili flakes
3 tablespoons sesame seeds, toasted
1 teaspoon soy sauce
2 teaspoons sesame oil
3 tablespoons peanut oil

Variation

For a more substantial meal, add a bundle of cooked Japanese noodles, such as udon, or strips of fried tempeh to the salad.

Pickled lotus root, arame and sesame salad

- 1 1/2 tablespoons arame (seaweed)
- 10 oz (300g) fresh or vacuum-packed lotus root, sliced paper thin
- 3 teaspoons superfine (caster) sugar
- 1 teaspoon sea salt
- 1/4 cup (2 fl oz / 60 ml) rice wine vinegar
- 1 tablespoon dark sesame oil
- 1/2 teaspoon plain black sesame seeds or toasted white sesame seeds
- 1 cup (1/2 oz / 15 g) pea shoots, washed
- pickled ginger, for garnish

Cover the arame with hot water and set aside for 20 minutes. Mix together the lotus root, sugar, salt and vinegar and set aside for 15 minutes. Drain the arame well. Add the arame to the lotus root mixture. Mix in the oil, sesame seeds and pea shoots. Divide between plates and garnish with a small amount of finely sliced pickled ginger. Serve on its own or with steamed rice.

Serves 2–4

Variation

Try thinly sliced cucumber or strips of blanched snow peas (mange-tout) in place of pea shoots. To make a more substantial meal, follow the salad with a nourishing bowl of miso soup and noodles.

Summer kim chee (Korean relish salad)

Steam the bok choy until just tender, about 2 minutes. Rinse under cold water and drain. Coarsely chop bases but leaves should remain whole. Peel the daikon, then using the peeler cut the daikon into long thin strips. Peel and seed the cucumber, then cut into strips to match the daikon strips. Combine the bok choy, daikon, cucumber, sprouts, ginger and garlic. Sprinkle with the salt, chili powder and sugar. Mix in the vinegar. Serve immediately or cover and refrigerate for 1 hour to allow the flavors to mingle. Serve on its own or with a bowl of rice and steamed greens.

Serves 4–8

- 1 bunch (13 oz / 400 g) bok choy, trimmed and quartered
- 1 medium daikon (white radish), 12 oz (375 g)
- 1 medium cucumber, 12 oz (375 g)
- 2 cups (2 oz / 60g) bean sprouts
- 2 tablespoons minced fresh ginger
- 3 cloves garlic, crushed
- 1 teaspoon salt
- 1/2 teaspoon dried chili powder
- 3 tablespoons superfine (caster) sugar
- 3 tablespoons white vinegar
- 2 tablespoons sesame salt (see page 13)

Savory sticky rice in banana leaves

- 1 cup (7 oz / 220 g) white or black glutinous (sticky) rice, soaked overnight in water
- pinch salt
- 1 cup (7 fl oz / 250 ml) thin coconut cream (see page 14), or half thick coconut cream and half water
- 2 kaffir lime leaves, finely sliced
- 2 tablespoons fried (French) shallots (see page 8)
- banana leaves cut into 4 lots of 6 inch (15 cm) squares, rinsed
- 4 pieces pandan leaves or string, for tying

Drain the rice after soaking. Mix with the salt, coconut cream and kaffir lime leaves. Pour into a heatproof bowl and cover tightly. Steam over boiling water until the liquid has evaporated, about 1 hour. Steam the banana leaves to soften and prevent splitting, about 2 minutes. Divide the rice into 4 portions and place 1 portion onto each banana leaf square. Top the rice with fried shallots and carefully wrap in the leaf. Secure with thin strips of pandan leaf or string. To reheat, steam for 15 minutes. Serve warm with vegetables or curry, or cold as a snack.

Serves 4

Steamed garlic chive and shiitake dumplings

In a bowl, combine the flours and salt. Mix the water and shortening in a saucepan and bring to a boil. Immediately pour the water mixture into the flour mixture and mix quickly using a wooden spoon. Press to form a smooth white dough. Roll into a thick cylinder and wrap in plastic. Set aside. In a bowl, mix all filling ingredients until combined. Unwrap and cut the dough into 20 pieces. Working 5 at a time so the dough does not dry out, flatten each piece to form a 4-inch (10-cm) round with the blade of a Chinese chopper or palette knife lightly brushed with sesame oil to prevent the dough from sticking. Divide the filling evenly between the dough pieces. Brush half the edge of each piece with sesame oil and fold each to form semi-circles. Crinkle and press the edges firmly together so they stick. Brush each dumpling with sesame oil. Steam on a piece of banana leaf or waxed paper for 15 minutes. Serve hot on fresh banana leaf with dipping sauce.

Makes 20

DUMPLING DOUGH

$^1/_2$ cup (2 oz / 60 g) Chinese wheat flour, sifted
$^1/_4$ cup (1 oz / 30 g) potato or corn starch flour, sifted
pinch salt
$^3/_4$ cup (4 fl oz / 125 ml) water
1 tablespoon solid vegetable shortening
sesame oil, for brushing
banana leaves, for serving
lemongrass, chili and soy dipping sauce (see page 14)

FILLING

12 dried shiitake mushrooms, soaked in hot water for 30 minutes, drained and finely chopped
4 tablespoons garlic chives, finely chopped
4 scallions (shallots / spring onions), finely chopped
2 teaspoons freshly grated ginger
1 clove garlic, minced
1 small red chili, seeded and finely chopped
$^2/_3$ cup (4 oz / 125 g) finely chopped water chestnuts
$^1/_2$ cup (3 oz / 95 g) finely chopped carrots
2 teaspoons potato or corn starch
$^1/_2$ teaspoon salt
1 teaspoon dark sesame oil
1 tablespoon soy sauce

Variation

In place of dough, use 20 gow gee wrappers.

Vegetarian "duck" pancakes

12 frozen Chinese pancakes, 5-inch (12.5-cm) diameter
$^1/_4$ cup (2 fl oz / 60 ml) vegetable oil
2 leeks, white part only julienned in 5-inch (12.5-cm) lengths
$^1/_2$ cup (30 oz / 90 g) water chestnuts, finely diced
7 oz (210 g) enoki mushrooms, uncut but torn into 12 bundles
6 teaspoons hoisin sauce

Defrost the pancakes and warm in a 225°F (110°C) oven for 10 minutes. Heat the oil in a large frying pan or wok over medium-high heat. Add the leek strips and cook, stirring to make sure they color evenly, until golden, 30–60 seconds. Remove and drain on paper towels. Increase the heat and add the chestnuts and enoki. Cook, stirring to color evenly, for 1 minute. Remove and drain on paper towels. Spread the pancakes on a flat work surface and spread ½ teaspoon of hoisin sauce on each. Divide the leek, chestnut and mushrooms evenly between the pancakes and roll them up. Serve immediately.

Makes 12

Variation

If pancakes are not readily available, substitute 12 trimmed iceberg lettuce leaves.

Mushroom and yellow bean noodles

Warm the oil in a medium frying pan or wok over medium-high heat. Add the garlic and onions and stir-fry until they just begin color, about 2 minutes. Increase the heat to high and add all the mushrooms. Stir them once to coat, then cook until you begin to smell them caramelizing, about 2 minutes. The important things here are to drive off the liquid and to fry rather than 'steam' the mushrooms. Stir again and continue to cook until there is no more liquid and the mushrooms are golden and rich, 2–3 minutes more. Add the bean and oyster sauces and reduce the heat to low. Cook gently for 1 minute more. While the mushrooms are cooking, drop the noodles into a pot of boiling salted water and simmer until tender, 4–5 minutes. Drain well. Cut the scallions into thin strips and plunge into ice water until they curl. Drain. Mix together scallions, cucumber, bell pepper and bean sprouts. Divide the noodles between individual bowls, top with the mushroom sauce and mixed vegetables.

Serves 4–8

1/4 cup (2 fl oz / 60 ml) peanut oil
2 cloves garlic, minced
1 small yellow onion, finely diced
1 lb (500 g) fresh mixed mushrooms, finely chopped
4 shiitake mushrooms, soaked in hot water for 30 minutes, drained and finely chopped
1/4 cup (2 fl oz / 60 ml) yellow (brown) bean sauce or black bean sauce
2 tablespoons vegetarian oyster (mushroom) sauce
1 lb (500 g) fresh Shanghai noodles
2 scallions (shallots / spring onions), green part only
1 small cucumber, peeled and julienned
1 small green bell pepper (capsicum), seeded and julienned
1 cup (2 oz / 60g) bean sprouts, steamed for 2 minutes and rinsed

Note

Shanghai noodles are available fresh in Asian food stores. They are thick like Hokkien noodles but, because they are made without eggs or coloring, they are white instead of yellow and are not oiled. If Shanghai noodles are unavailable, substitute any thick plain noodles, fresh or dried.

Deep-fried garlic chive wontons

15 round wonton wrappers
15 garlic chives, cut into 1-inch (2.5-cm) lengths
4 teaspoons ginger sesame dressing (see page 13)
vegetable oil, for deep frying
chili sambal (see page 22), sweet chili sauce or soy sauce, for serving

Separate the wonton wrappers and lay on a work surface. Arrange the garlic chives in the center of each wrapper. Top each with ¼ teaspoon of ginger sesame dressing. Brush the edges of each wrapper with water, fold and press the edges together firmly. Heat a minimum of 2 inches (5 cm) oil in a deep fryer or medium-large, heavy-based pot until the temperature reaches 350°F (175°C). Carefully lower five wontons at a time into the hot oil and cook until pale golden and crisp, about 2 minutes. Turn them over halfway through cooking. Remove from the oil and drain on paper towels. Keep warm while frying the remaining wontons. Serve hot with sambal, sweet chili sauce or soy sauce for dipping.

Makes 15

Noodles with enoki mushrooms, sesame and soy

Heat ¾ inch (2 cm) vegetable oil in a wok until hot. Add celery leaves, a few at a time, and cook just until they become transparent, about 15–30 seconds. Remove from the oil, drain and continue until all the leaves are fried. Leaves will stay crisp for at least 2 hours.

Slice the noodles into roughly 1-inch (2.5-cm) strips. Cover them with boiling water and carefully separate them using a fork or chopsticks. When separate, soak for 5–10 minutes, drain, rinse, and drain thoroughly. Gently stir ½ teaspoon peanut oil through the noodles to prevent sticking. Set aside.

Warm the 2 tablespoons peanut oil in a medium frying pan or wok over high heat. Add the sprouts, the mushrooms, scallions and celery slices. Cook until the vegetables just begin to collapse, about 4 minutes. Add the noodles, sesame oil, soy and oyster sauces. Gently stir to combine and transfer to individual bowls. Sprinkle with sesame seeds and fried celery leaves. Serve with extra soy sauce.

Serves 4–6

4 celery sticks, flesh sliced on an angle, and leaves
vegetable oil, for frying
1 lb (500 g) fresh rice sheet noodles
½ teaspoon plus 2 tablespoons peanut oil
2 cups (4 oz / 120 g) bean sprouts
4 oz (125 g) enoki mushrooms
4 oz (125 g) oyster (abalone) or button mushrooms
2 scallions (shallots / spring onions), finely sliced on an angle
1 tablespoon dark sesame oil
1 tablespoon soy sauce plus extra, for serving
2 tablespoons oyster (mushroom) sauce
2 teaspoons sesame seeds, toasted or gomasio (see page 13)
soy sauce, for serving

Stir-fried egg noodles with vegetables (Mi goreng)

10 oz (300 g) thin dried egg noodles
$^1/_4$ cup (2 fl oz / 60 ml) peanut oil
2 cloves garlic, minced
1 medium yellow onion, finely sliced into half moons
2 celery sticks, finely sliced on an angle
3 cups (6 oz / 180 g) shredded Chinese cabbage
1 cup (6 oz / 185 g) baby corn, halved lengthwise
1 medium red bell pepper (capsicum), seeded and sliced into thin strips
2 tablespoons ketjap manis (sweet soy sauce), plus extra for serving
1 tablespoon soy sauce
2 medium eggs, beaten
2 scallions (shallots / spring onions), finely sliced on an angle

Drop the noodles into a large pot of boiling, salted water, return to a boil and cook until tender, about 4 minutes. Drain and rinse in cold water. Set aside. Warm the oil in a large frying pan or wok over medium-high heat. Add the garlic and onion, and stir-fry until they begin to color, about 2 minutes. Increase the heat and add the celery, cabbage, corn and bell pepper and continue cooking until the vegetables soften, about 4 minutes. Add the noodles and both types of soy sauce and stir well to combine. Add the beaten eggs and fold gently so the eggs just cook, about 1 minute. Transfer to individual bowls. Sprinkle with scallions. Serve with extra ketjap manis.

Serves 6–8

Variation

Top each serving with a single fried egg. Alternatively, pour the beaten egg into a lightly oiled non-stick frying pan over medium heat and swirl around to form a single, very thin coating. After 1 minute, turn the omelette and color on the other side. Invert onto a work surface, roll up quickly and slice thinly. Divide between the bowls.

Peanut-spiced beans with turmeric rice

To make turmeric rice: Place all the rice ingredients into a large pot and bring to a boil. Reduce the heat to the lowest possible setting, stir and cover the pot tightly. Simmer until the rice is tender and the liquid absorbed, about 30 minutes. When cooked, remove from the heat and fluff the rice using a fork.

Steam the beans and sweet potato until tender and set aside. Warm the oil in a medium frying pan or wok over medium-high heat. Add the garlic, onion and chili. Stir-fry until the ingredients begin to color, about 2 minutes. Stir in the salt, lemon juice, ketjap manis, peanuts, tamarind paste, sugar and beans. Add a tablespoon of water if the mix looks too dry. Stir in the sweet potato and cook over low heat for 2 minutes more. Divide the rice and beans among individual plates. Garnish with the shallots.

Serves 6–8

TURMERIC RICE

1½ cups (10½ oz / 330 g) jasmine rice
2 cups (16 fl oz / 500 ml) vegetable stock
1½ cups (12 fl oz / 375 ml) thin coconut cream (see page 14)
1 kaffir lime leaf, finely sliced
1 piece fresh turmeric, 1 inch (2.5 cm), grated, or 1 teaspoon dried turmeric
2 teaspoons salt

15 oz (450 g) yard long (snake) or green beans, cut into 4-inch (10-cm) lengths
1 sweet potato, 12 oz (360 g), peeled and diced
2 tablespoons peanut oil
3 cloves garlic, minced
1 yellow onion, finely chopped
3 small red chili peppers, seeded and finely sliced
½ teaspoon salt
1 tablespoon lemon juice
1 tablespoon kecap manis (sweet soy sauce)
¼ cup (1½ oz / 45 g) roasted and coarsely chopped peanuts
1 tablespoon tamarind paste
1 tablespoon grated palm sugar
¼ cup (2 oz / 60 g) fried (French) shallots

Beijing noodles with pea shoots and black vinegar

- 17 oz (500 g) fresh or dried Chinese wheat noodles
- 1 tablespoon dark sesame oil
- 1/4 cup (2 fl oz / 60 ml) peanut oil
- 4 shallots (French), finely sliced
- 4 cloves garlic, crushed
- 6 oz (180 g) lotus root, thinly sliced
- pinch salt
- 3 tablespoons Chinese black vinegar
- 6 cups (3 oz / 90 g) pea shoots
- 1/4 cup (2 fl oz / 60 ml) vegetarian oyster (mushroom) sauce
- 5 scallions (shallots / spring onions), finely sliced on an angle
- chili, black vinegar and sesame dressing (see page 14)

Drop the noodles into a large pot of salted, boiling water and boil for 1 minute. Drain the noodles and toss with sesame oil to prevent the strands from sticking. Keep warm. Warm a wok over medium-high heat and add the peanut oil. Add the shallots and garlic and stir-fry briskly until they begin to color, about 1 minute. Add the lotus root, and stir-fry until it begins to color, about 3 minutes. Add the salt, black vinegar, and hot noodles. Reduce the heat to medium-low. Add the pea shoots and stir gently so the heat of the noodles causes the pea shoots to wilt, about 2 minutes. Stir in the oyster sauce. Divide among individual hot bowls and garnish with scallions. Serve with chili, black vinegar and sesame dressing for dipping.

Serves 4–6

Hokkien noodles with black bean sauce

Cover the noodles with boiling water and set aside for 2 minutes. Drain. Warm the oil in a large frying pan or wok over medium-high heat. Add the garlic and shallots and stir-fry until they just begin to color, about 30 seconds. Add the baby corn, mushrooms, bok choy and choy sum. Sprinkle on the water, drizzle on the black bean sauce and spread the noodles on top. Cover and simmer for 3–5 minutes, depending on how crunchy you like your vegetables. Remove from the heat, and stir well. Divide among individual bowls. Sprinkle with the fried shallots and fresh chili if desired.

Serves 4–6

- 1$^1/_4$ lb (625 g) fresh or vacuum-packed hokkien noodles
- 3 tablespoons vegetable oil
- 4 cloves garlic, crushed
- 2 shallots (French), finely chopped
- 1 cup (6 oz / 185 g) baby corn, halved lengthwise
- 4 oz (125 g) oyster (abalone) mushrooms, coarsely chopped
- $^1/_2$ bunch (6 oz / 185 g) bok choy, halved lengthwise
- $^1/_2$ bunch (6 oz / 185 g) choy sum
- $^1/_4$ cup (2 fl oz / 60 ml) water
- $^1/_4$ cup (2 fl oz / 60 ml) black bean sauce
- fried (French) shallots for garnish, optional
- chopped fresh red chili pepper for garnish, optional

Laksa with vegetables and tofu puffs

- 2 tablespoons vegetable oil
- 4 stalks lemongrass, bases crushed
- 4 small red chili peppers, seeded and finely sliced
- 4 cloves garlic, minced
- 1 piece fresh tumeric, 1 inch (2.5 cm), grated, or 3/4 teaspoon dried turmeric
- 1 piece fresh galangal, 2 inch (5 cm), peeled and finely sliced
- 1 medium (3 oz / 90 g) carrot, julienned
- 1 tablespoon grated palm sugar
- 2 tablespoons tamarind paste
- 2 tablespoons lime juice
- 4 cups (32 fl oz / 1 L) thin coconut cream (see page 14)
- 2 cups (16 fl oz / 500 ml) water
- 7 oz (210 g) tofu (bean curd) puffs
- 8 oz (250 g) fresh thin rice noodles
- 7 oz (210 g) snow peas (mange tout), trimmed and steamed until tender
- 2 cups (4 oz / 125 g) bean sprouts
- 1 red bell pepper (capsicum), seeded and finely julienned
- 2 cups (1 oz / 30 g) pea shoots, rinsed
- 1/2 cup (1/2 oz / 15 g) cilantro (coriander) leaves
- 4–6 tablespoons fried (French) shallots (see page 8)

Warm the oil in a large saucepan over medium-high heat. Add the lemongrass, chili peppers, garlic, turmeric, galangal and carrot. Stir-fry until the mix begins to color, about 3 minutes. Add the sugar, tamarind, lime juice, coconut cream, water and tofu. Bring to a boil, reduce the heat to a simmer and cook, uncovered, for 15 minutes. While this is cooking, bring a large pot of water to a boil and cook the noodles until tender, 3–5 minutes depending on their thickness. Drain and rinse well. Divide the noodles among individual bowls. Spoon over the liquid. Top each bowl with the snow peas, bean sprouts, bell pepper, pea shoots, cilantro and a sprinkle of fried shallots.

Serves 4–6

Vegetables and spiced coconut steamed in banana leaves

Warm the oil in a medium frying pan or wok over medium-high heat. Add the eggplant and bell pepper and stir-fry until the vegetables begin to color, about 3 minutes. Add the bean sprouts and curry paste and stir well. Fold in the coconut cream and simmer for 2 minutes. Add the cilantro leaves. Soften the banana leaf squares and strips in a steamer to prevent splitting, 3–5 minutes. Place the banana leaves on a work surface. Divide the rice between each leaf and top with the vegetable mix. Fold over the sides of the banana leaf to enclose mixture and secure with strips of banana leaf. Steam for 20 minutes. Open packets to serve. Garnish with the coconut.

Serves 4–8

2 tablespoons vegetable oil
13 oz (400 g) baby eggplant, halved lengthwise then cut into thin strips
1 medium red bell pepper (capsicum), seeded and julienned
1 cup (1 oz / 30 g) bean sprouts
2 tablespoons hot or mild vegetarian Masaman or other curry paste
1 cup (8 fl oz / 250 ml) thin coconut cream (see page 14)
1/2 cup (1/2 oz / 15 g) cilantro (coriander) leaves
8 squares banana leaf, each 10 inches (25 cm)
8 strips banana leaf, pandan leaf, string or toothpicks, for tying
2 cups (10 oz / 300 g) steamed white rice
2 tablespoons flaked coconut, toasted

Thai red-curried tofu puffs and vegetables

1 tablespoon vegetable oil
2–3 tablespoons Thai red curry paste, or other vegetarian curry paste
2 medium (6 oz / 180 g) carrots, julienned
4 oz (125 g) bamboo shoots, julienned
1 medium red bell pepper (capsicum), seeded and julienned
7 oz (210 g) tofu (bean curd) puffs
1½ cups (12 fl oz / 375 ml) thin coconut cream (see page 14)
1 cup (8 fl oz / 250 ml) water
2 kaffir lime leaves, finely sliced
zest of 1 kaffir lime
2 cups (1 oz / 30 g) pea shoots, rinsed and cut in half
steamed rice, for serving (optional)
½ cup (½ oz / 15 g) cilantro (coriander) leaves

Warm the oil in a deep-frying pan or wok over medium-high heat. Add the curry paste and stir-fry for 1 minute to release the aromas. Add the carrot, bamboo, bell pepper and tofu. Stir in the coconut cream, water, lime leaves and zest. Cover the pan and simmer for 20 minutes. Stir in the pea shoots. Transfer to a serving dish or divide among individual plates and serve over steamed rice. Garnish with fresh cilantro leaves.

Serves 4–6

Variation

Try curry pastes from different countries for a range of flavors.

Claypot-cooked vegetables with shiitake and Chinese five-spice

Soak a Chinese claypot in water for an hour before using. Alternatively, use a casserole dish. Preheat oven to 400°F (200°C). Mix all the ingredients together and place in the cooking container. Put the pot in a large baking dish filled with enough water to reach halfway up the pot. Bake for 1 hour. Serve from the claypot at the table. Accompany with steamed rice.

Serves 4–8

2 tablespoons vegetable oil
12 dried shiitake mushrooms, soaked in hot water for 30 minutes, drained and finely chopped
2 cloves garlic, minced
1 medium yellow onion, sliced into half moons
4 cups (20 oz / 600 g) mixed fresh vegetables such as pumpkin, cauliflower, carrot, eggplant, baby corn, cut into 1-inch (2.5-cm) cubes
2 teaspoons Chinese five-spice powder
2 tablespoons brown sugar
1 cup (8 fl oz / 250 ml) clear vegetable stock
2 tablespoons vegetarian oyster (mushroom) sauce
1 bunch (15 oz / 450 g) choy sum or bok choy, quartered lengthwise
steamed rice, for serving

Tempeh marinated in chili and soy

- 8 oz (250 g) tempeh, cut into $^1/_6$-inch (4-mm) slices
- 2 tablespoons soy sauce
- 1 tablespoon ketjap manis (sweet soy sauce)
- 1 medium yellow onion, sliced into half moons
- $7^1/_2$ oz (225 g) yard long (snake) or green beans, cut into 2-inch (5-cm) lengths
- 1 teaspoon freshly grated ginger
- 2 cloves garlic, minced
- 1 tablespoon grated palm sugar
- 1–2 small red chili peppers, seeded and finely sliced
- 2 tablespoons vegetable oil, plus extra if required
- $^1/_4$ cup ($^1/_4$ oz / 7 g) chopped cilantro (coriander)
- steamed rice, for serving

In a bowl, combine the tempeh, soy sauce, ketjap manis, onion, beans, ginger, garlic, sugar and chili peppers. Cover and marinate for 1 hour. Remove only the tempeh strips from the marinade. Warm the oil in a medium frying pan or wok over medium-high heat. Add the tempeh strips and fry until golden on both sides, about 4 minutes. Remove from the pan and set aside to keep warm. Pour the vegetables and marinade into the pan or wok. Add 1 teaspoon more oil if required. Stir-fry until golden and cooked, about 5 minutes. Divide the vegetables and tempeh strips among individual plates. Garnish with the cilantro. Accompany with steamed rice.

Serves 4–6

Spicy breadfruit and lotus chips with fried basil

Warm the oil in a deep fryer or well-stabilized wok until it reaches 350°F (175°C) on a deep-frying thermometer. Carefully place a quarter of the fruit and vegetable slices into the oil and cook until the bubbles disperse and the pieces are pale golden, about 1–2 minutes. Remove and drain on paper towels. Continue with the remaining batches. Working in 2 batches, fry the basil leaves until transparent, about 15–30 seconds. Toss together basil and fruit and vegetable chips. Serve the chips sprinkled with Szechuan pepper and salt or sambal.

Serves 2–4 as a snack

8 oz (250 g) mix of breadfruit, lotus root and green banana, all peeled and thinly sliced
8 oz (250 g) mix of sweet potato, yam and plain potato, all unpeeled and thinly sliced
vegetable oil for deep frying
1 cup (1 oz / 30 g) basil leaves
Szechuan pepper and salt mix (see page 14) or chili sambal (see page 15), to taste

Note

When the deep-frying oil is cool, strain and reuse for up to 1 week.

Variation

Fried snack foods are readily available throughout South East Asia. Any starchy fruit or vegetable is suitable for frying. Try mixing the vegetable snacks with freshly fried cassava crackers, a vegetarian version of popular prawn crackers.

Cabbage nori rolls

- 1 Chinese cabbage, cut lengthwise into 16 wedges
- pinch salt
- 2 medium (6 oz / 185 g) carrots, peeled and julienned
- 8 nori (seaweed) sheets
- 1 avocado, peeled and cut into slivers
- 1 small cucumber, peeled and julienned
- 2 tablespoons gari (pickled ginger) (see page 13)
- 1 tablespoon ponzu (Japanese citrus soy), or other soy sauce
- 2 teaspoons wasabi paste

Sprinkle the cabbage wedges with salt. Steam the cabbage and carrots until tender, about 5 minutes. Cool completely. Roll two cabbage wedges at a time in a bamboo sushi mat or kitchen cloth to wring out excess moisture. Toast the nori sheets over a low flame until they change color, about 30 seconds for each side. Lay a nori sheet on a bamboo mat or work surface. Divide the cabbage, carrot, avocado and cucumber evenly between each sheet. Using your index finger and thumb, pick up the edge of the mat nearest you and roll forward, tightly wrapping the nori around the vegetables. Unroll the mat and place the roll on a chopping board with the seam on the bottom. Repeat with remaining sheets. Allow each roll to set for a few minutes. Wipe a knife with a damp cloth and cut each roll into 6–8 pieces. Serve with ginger, soy and wasabi.

Serves 6–8

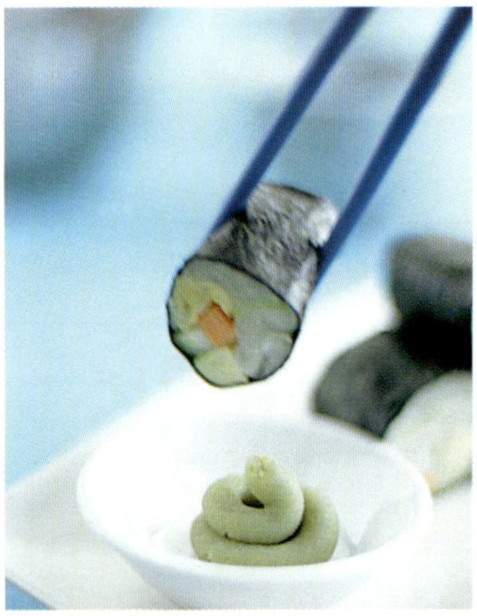

Variation

For a more substantial snack, add thin slices of tofu or pan-fried tempeh to the roll. Add a dollop of Japanese mayonnaise to each slice of nori before serving.

Red-cooked tofu and vegetables

Drain the tofu and pat dry with paper towels. Warm the oil in a pot just large enough to contain all the ingredients. Put the single block of tofu in the pot and sear on all sides, about 2 minutes total. Add the remaining ingredients except the sesame oil and scallions. Bring to a boil, cover tightly and simmer for 20 minutes. Turn over the tofu, stir and simmer, covered, for 20 minutes more. Remove the pot from the heat and set aside to cool completely and allow the tofu and vegetables to absorb all the flavors of the sauce, about 1 hour. Reheat the dish to simmer for 2 minutes. Remove the tofu, brush with the sesame oil and carve into slices. Divide rice among individual plates. Top with tofu then vegetables, sauce and scattered scallions.

Serves 4–8

24 oz (750 g) firm tofu (bean curd)
2 tablespoons peanut oil
1 medium yellow onion, sliced into half moons
2 cloves garlic, minced
4 cups (20 oz / 600 g) mixed fresh vegetables such as pumpkin, baby corn, eggplant, mushrooms, carrots
4 teaspoons Chinese five-spice powder
1/4 cup (2 oz / 60 g) brown sugar
4 teaspoons freshly grated ginger
1 1/2 cups (12 fl oz / 375 ml) water
1 1/2 cups (12 fl oz / 375 ml) dark soy sauce
1/2 cup (4 fl oz / 125 ml) rice wine vinegar or dry sherry
2 teaspoons sesame oil
steamed rice, for serving
4 scallions (shallots / spring onions), finely sliced and curled in ice water (see page 17)

Note

Freeze any excess sauce and add to the recipe the next time you make it to contribute a richer flavor.

Chili pepper omelette with pea shoots and soy

6 medium eggs
$^1/_4$ cup (2 fl oz / 60 ml) milk
pinch salt
1 teaspoon chili sambal (see page 15)
or $^1/_2$–1 teaspoon chili pepper flakes
2 teaspoons peanut oil
1 cup (1 oz / 30 g) pea shoots
2 teaspoons soy sauce

In a bowl, whisk together the eggs, milk, salt and sambal. Warm the oil in a large, non-stick frying pan or wok over medium-high heat. Add the egg mixture and immediately swirl around so that the egg spreads over as much of the surface area as possible. Continue gently swirling until all the liquid sets. When the egg frills around the edges, about 4 minutes, spread the pea shoots over the surface and sprinkle with the soy sauce. Roll up quickly, turn out the omelette and cut into ½-inch (12-mm) thick slices. Serve the omelette hot by itself, on top of steamed rice or as a cold snack, with extra sambal and soy sauce.

Serves 2–4

Variation

Instead of pea shoots, try steamed spinach or bean sprouts.

Nori-wrapped mochi with radish and soy

In a medium pot, combine the rice with the water, ginger and salt. Cover and simmer on the gentlest possible heat until all the liquid is absorbed and the rice is quite stiff, 1–1½ hours. Alternatively, cook in a pressure cooker for 20–30 minutes. Transfer to a large metal bowl and pound with either a pestle or the end of a rolling pin to crush the grains of rice. Occasionally dip the end of the pestle or pin in water to prevent it from sticking to the rice. When the grains are crushed and a very stiff paste forms, divide the dough into 8 pieces. Using moistened hands, form each piece into a ball or a square about 2 inches (5 cm) in size. Wrap a single strip of nori around each ball or square, moistening the edges of the nori with water to secure it in place. Mix together the radish, soy sauce and ginger and serve on top of each piece.

Serves 4–8

- 3 cups (21 oz / 660 g) glutinous (sticky) rice, soaked in water overnight and drained
- 5 cups (40 fl oz / 1250 ml) water
- 1 teaspoon grated ginger
- ¼ teaspoon salt
- 1 nori seaweed sheet, cut into 8 strips
- ½ cup grated daikon (white radish) or red radish
- 1 tablespoon shoyu (Japanese soy sauce)
- 2 teaspoons gari (pickled ginger), finely sliced (see page 13)

Note

Easy to digest, mochi is widely eaten in Japan as a traditional strengthening food for people recovering from illness, to treat anemia and to stimulate milk production in nursing mothers.

Variation

Roll mochi balls in toasted ground walnuts instead of nori.

Stir-fried Asian greens with vegetarian oyster sauce

1 bunch (16 oz / 500 g) gai larn (Chinese broccoli) or broccolini
pinch salt
2 teaspoons vegetable oil
pinch superfine (caster) sugar
2 tablespoons vegetarian oyster (mushroom) sauce
2 tablespoons hot water
3 tablespoons fried (French) shallots, optional (see page 8)

Cut the gai larn into 4-inch (10-cm) lengths. To keep the vegetable intact and allow for more even cooking, slice the stalks lengthwise towards the thinner ends without cutting all the way through. Lay the gai larn flat in a steamer, sprinkle with the salt and steam until tender but still crisp, about 3 minutes. Warm the oil in a medium frying pan or wok over medium-high heat. Add the gai larn. Sprinkle with the sugar, oyster sauce and water. Bring to a simmer. As soon as sauce simmers, remove from the heat. Serve immediately, sprinkled with the shallots. Accompany with steamed rice.

Serves 4

Variation

Substitute gai larn with choy sum, bok choy, spinach, snow pea shoots or asparagus.

Braised flowering chives with ginger

Trim about 1 inch (2.5 cm) from the bases and tops of the chives. Warm the oil in a medium frying pan or wok over medium-high heat. Add the garlic, ginger and bell pepper and stir-fry until they begin to color, about 1 minute. Add the chives and toss for 1 minute more. Add the remaining ingredients and simmer until the sauce is thick and clear, about 2 minutes. Serve immediately, on its own or with steamed rice.

Serves 4–6

- 2 bunches flowering chives
- 2 tablespoons vegetable oil
- 2 cloves garlic, minced
- 2 teaspoons freshly grated ginger
- 1 small green bell pepper (capsicum), seeded and julienned
- 1 teaspoon sesame oil
- 2 tablespoons soy sauce
- 1 teaspoon corn starch, dissolved in 3 tablespoons water

Variation

Substitute other green vegetables for chives such as yard long (snake) beans, spinach, choy sum or bok choy.

Almond jelly with pandan and lychees

3 cups (24 fl oz / 750 ml) water
1 cup ($5^{1}/_{2}$ oz / 170 g) whole almonds, blanched
2 pandan leaves
$^{1}/_{2}$ cup (4 oz / 125 g) grated palm sugar
2 teaspoons agar-agar powder
$^{1}/_{2}$ teaspoon almond extract (essence)
1 mango, peeled and pureed
12 fresh lychees, peeled
watermelon (optional)

Blend 2 cups (16 fl oz / 500 ml) of the water with the almonds and set aside for 3 minutes or until smooth. Press the almond mixture through a fine sieve to extract as much of the liquid as possible. This is almond milk. Bring the remaining water to a boil. Add the pandan leaves, sugar and agar-agar, stirring constantly until the agar-agar dissolves. Add the almond milk to the sugar mixture and stir. Remove and discard the pandan. Pour the syrup into individual lightly oiled molds or a single large mold about 4 cups (32 fl oz / 1 L) in size. Cover and refrigerate until set, about 1 hour. Serve with the mango puree and fruit.

Serves 6

Note

Asian jellies are usually very firm, unlike their Western counterparts. If you prefer a softer texture, reduce the amount of agar-agar powder.

Variation

Substitute two kaffir lime leaves for the pandan leaves and vary the fruit served with the jelly.

Coconut milk and rose flower sorbet

Combine the coconut powder and sugars. Whisk in the water. Bring to a boil, stirring occasionally. Watch it carefully because it will quickly boil over. Immediately remove from the heat and add the rose flower water. Refrigerate for 30 minutes or until chilled. Churn in an ice cream machine according to the manufacturer's instructions, or pour into a plastic container and freeze until solid, periodically whisking the partially frozen sorbet to break up the ice crystals and give a smoother result. When completely frozen, serve in chilled glasses or bowls scattered with the rose petals or the toasted coconut.

Serves 4

6 oz (180 g) dried coconut powder
1/4 cup (2 oz / 60 g) superfine (caster) sugar
1/4 cup (2 oz / 60 g) grated palm sugar
1 1/2 cups (12 fl oz / 375 ml) water
1/4 cup (2 fl oz / 60 ml) rose flower water
edible rose petals, for garnish
toasted coconut (optional)

Variation

Replace the rose flower water with 4 tablespoons of fresh mango puree and garnish the sorbet with mango slices.

Japanese green tea ice cream

$^{3}/_{4}$ cup (6 fl oz / 180 ml) milk
2 oz (60 g) powdered green tea ice cream base
1 medium egg, beaten
red bean paste (see page 15), optional

In a small pot, bring milk to a boil. Remove from the heat and whisk into the green tea powder. Add the egg. Return the mix to the pot. Cook over medium heat until the mix begins to thicken slightly, 1–2 minutes. Do not boil or the egg will separate. Remove from the heat, strain and chill over an iced bowl. Freeze until solid. Remove from the freezer to soften a little before serving. Divide among individual bowls. Top with red bean paste if desired.

Serves 2–4

Note

Green tea ice cream powder is available from Asian food shops that stock predominantly Japanese goods. Using the powder is the most common way of making this very popular dessert at home.

Sticky rice pudding with tropical fruit

Drain and rinse the soaked rice. Place in a heavy-based pot. Add the water and pandan leaves. Bring to a boil, cover and reduce the heat to a simmer. Cook until very tender, about 30 minutes. Remove from the heat, add the sugar and salt and stir until dissolved. To serve, either spoon into individual bowls, or form into balls using wet hands and place on serving plates. Arrange the fruit next to the rice and top with the coconut cream. Garnish with the grated coconut if desired.

Serves 4–6

- 1½ cups (10 oz / 330 g) black or white glutinous (sticky) rice, soaked overnight in water
- 2 cups (16 fl oz / 500 ml) water
- 2 pandan leaves
- 1 cup (8 oz / 250 g) grated palm sugar
- ½ teaspoon salt
- 1½ cups (7 oz / 225 g) peeled and sliced mixed tropical fruit
- ½ cup (4 fl oz / 125 ml) thick coconut cream (see page 14) or freshly grated coconut
- ½ cup (2 oz / 60 g) fresh grated coconut, optional

Variation

In Thailand this dish would be served with steamed corn kernels and young fresh coconut flesh instead of fruit.

Indonesian sweet potato and coconut drink (kolak)

1 sweet potato (12 oz / 375 g), peeled and cubed
3$^1/_2$ cups (28 fl oz / 875 ml) water
$^1/_2$ cup (4 oz / 125 g) grated palm sugar
1 pandan leaf, folded, or 2 kaffir lime leaves, finely sliced
2 tablespoons sweet potato flour or tapioca balls, cooked until translucent
$^1/_2$ cup (4 fl oz / 125 ml) thin coconut cream (see page 14)

Place the sweet potato in a pot and cover with water. Add the palm sugar and pandan leaf and bring to a boil. Simmer until tender, about 20 minutes. Remove from the heat and stir in the potato flour balls and coconut cream. Serve in glasses as a drink, either hot or over ice.

Serves 2–4

Note

Non-alcoholic drinks are an art form in Asia and infinitely more varied than a milkshake or flavored soda.

Variation

These drinks are often served hot or cold over ice in place of dessert or as a sweet mini-meal throughout the day. Many are coconut based. Shaved iced sweetened with fruit syrup and fresh fruit or sweet beans is common, as are blended avocado drinks, tea, sweetened soy beverages and iced drinks featuring floating jelly-like lumps of various fruit and vegetable starches.

Broiled pineapple with tamarind and coconut

Put the palm sugar and water in a small pot and bring to a boil. Reduce the heat to simmer and cook, uncovered, for 2 minutes. Add the tamarind and chili pepper and simmer for 3 minutes more, breaking up the tamarind with the back of a wooden spoon. Press the mixture through a sieve and set aside. Cut the pineapple lengthwise into 8 wedges, leaving the core of the pineapple in if it is young and tender. Skewer each piece of pineapple along the length of the wedge. Coat well with the tamarind syrup. Broil (grill) the pineapple until it is golden, about 2 minutes on each side. Transfer to banana leaves, if using, placed on a platter or individual plate. Serve with coconut cream over the top or on the side.

Serves 4

- 1/2 cup (2 oz / 60 g) grated palm sugar
- 1/2 cup (4 fl oz / 125 ml) water
- 2 tablespoons unsalted tamarind pulp
- 1 small red chili pepper, halved
- 1 whole pineapple, about 2 lb (1kg), peeled
- 8 bamboo skewers, soaked in cold water for 30 minutes
- 4 banana leaves, optional
- 1/4 cup (2 fl oz / 60 ml) thick coconut cream (see page 14)

Variations

Try this recipe with other firm fruit, such as banana or mango. You could also use lemongrass sticks as skewers. Add ice and club soda to the tamarind syrup for a refreshing drink.

STEP-BY-STEP

making tea

Preparing and serving tea is an art form in many Asian countries. The quality of both the tea leaves and ceramic tea pots and cups are exquisitely varied. The water temperatures, leaf quantities and methods of preparation are complex and culturally specific.

Step 1

Fill a teapot with boiling water to warm the pot, then drain completely and dry.

Step 2

Measure whole tea leaves (black, green, oolong, or flower-scented) into the pot. You will need 1 teaspoon per 1 cup (8 fl oz / 250 ml) water.

Step 3

Boil in a kettle the required amount of water plus 1 cup (8 fl oz / 250 ml) extra. As soon as it boils, remove from the heat. Pour the extra water onto the leaves, swirl them around, and discard the water. Pour the remaining water onto the leaves and steep for 1 minute.

Step 4

Pour into cups from a height to cool the tea slightly and cause it to froth. Make sure all the water is drained from the leaves.

glossary

Agar-agar: This is the vegetarian equivalent of the setting agent gelatin, which is derived from boiled hooves. Agar-agar derives from seaweed, and is both colorless and odorless. Available from health food stores in strands, flakes or powder form, it is known in Japan as kanten and is used to set both sweet and savory dishes. It is more effective than gelatin, so if you are converting a dish use less by volume. Dissolve in water before adding to a dish. Agar-agar will not set jellies containing alcohol very effectively.

Braising: This technique is more frequently used to cook poorer quality cuts of meat. However, it is also useful for some vegetable dishes, especially those that include the soy products tofu and tempeh. The food to be braised is first browned in hot oil, which creates a rich flavor. Liquid and other flavorings are then added and the dish is covered and cooked for a long period in the oven. The flavors melt together and the dish remains moist and tender, tasting quite different to either steamed or stir-fried food.

Chinese red-cooking: This cooking method relies on the combined flavors of light and dark soy sauce, Chinese five-spice, sherry and brown sugar. Surround meats, poultry, vegetables, and firm tofu (bean curd) with the sauce, cook then set aside to cool. The foods take on the intense color and flavor of the sauce. Brush with sesame oil before serving. Keep any excess sauce frozen and add to the next red-cooked dish. This is a common practice in China, where a master red sauce may be generations old.

Cooking oils: Asian food is often cooked in neutral vegetable oils. The most stable oils are sunflower, soy and safflower. Corn and rapeseed oils are good value, but check that they are not from genetically modified crops. Peanut oil is popular, but, as with all nut oils, has a short shelf life. Coconut oil, although common, is unfortunately high in saturated fats, which makes it a very unhealthy choice. Almond oil has an excellent flavor for brushing dessert molds for jellies and custards. Sesame oil is dark (from toasted seeds) or light (from untoasted seeds). Dark sesame is very strongly flavored and burns easily if heated too much. For deep-frying, choose an inexpensive neutral oil; dress salads and cook stir-fries with peanut oil.

Deep-frying: In an ideal world, every kitchen would have a proper deep-fryer with a thermostat. Asian cooks, however, do an enormous amount of frying without one. Their secret is a wok. It must be very well stabilized, and the frying oil should be no more than 2 inches (5 cm) deep. Heating to the correct temperature takes just a couple of minutes. To test, carefully put in a thin slice of potato. If it sinks to the bottom, the oil is not yet hot enough; if it bubbles around the edges and floats, the oil is probably about right; if the potato starts to smoke or turns instantly black, the oil is too hot and should be immediately removed from the heat because it may catch fire. Some cooks use a sprinkling of flour instead of potato to check the temperature of the oil. Frequent cooks should have no problem mastering this alternative deep-frying technique, but if there is any doubt, get a proper deep-fryer.

Legumes: A legume is any plant that has a seed-bearing pod. There are over 12,000 plants that fit this description including lentils, peas, beans, peanuts, tamarind and alfalfa. Pulse is the correct name for the edible dried seeds of leguminous plants. Legumes are an excellent source of non-animal protein for vegetarians all over the world. They often require soaking before cooking, but using a pressure cooker will reduce the cooking times and pre-cooked varieties are also available.

Noodles: The variety of noodles available in Asia could easily fill a book. In most cases when a specific type of noodle is called for, it's best to look for that type. If it is not available fresh, look for a dry version, or vice versa. Or, find a similar noodle type from the same country or region—chances are it will have similar flavors. Substituting across countries or regions is not usually a good idea: a dish requiring Japanese soba noodles, for example, will not have the right flavors to match a hokkien noodle dish.

Soy and soybean sauces: Soy sauce is made from fermented soybeans. The most basic distinction is whether it is light or dark, with the saltier light types most commonly served as a table condiment and the sweeter, dark version used in cooking. However, there are many different varieties. Ponzu is a Japanese citrus soy, ketjap manis is an Indonesian sweet soy, tamari is a by-product of making miso, shoyu is a Japanese soy aged for 1–2 years, mushroom soy is flavored with straw mushrooms, and there are other types specific to different countries. Soybean sauces include yellow bean (fermented yellow soybeans), black bean (fermented black soybeans) and hoisin (soybean sauce flavored with garlic, chili and sesame). Reduced salt versions of some of these sauces are also available.

Steaming: This cooking technique is one of the easiest to master. It does not matter how hard or long water is boiled for, the boiling temperature will always be the same. This means that unlike the more variable baking or frying techniques, food being steamed can never brown or burn. It is a very important technique for a lot of Asian food and a steamer is one of the few utensils found in most kitchens. The important points to remember are that the water in the base of the steamer must not boil dry, and the lid must be tightly secured to contain the steam.

Stir-frying: This is a very common cooking technique across Asia. It requires a wok or fry pan over a moderately high heat, a little vegetable oil and finely chopped fresh vegetables which then form the base of an infinite variety of dishes. The hot oil causes the stir-frying food to brown and produces their characteristic rich flavors. The interior of the vegetables should remain crisp and moist. Once the ingredients are cut, stir-frying is a fast and convenient way to prepare many different foods.

Vegetarian (oyster) mushroom sauce: Vegetarian versions are available for many common Asian sauces. Standard oyster sauce is flavored with dried oyster extract. The vegetarian version is flavored with mushroom extract. Since both will be labeled "oyster sauce", it is best to read the ingredient list to be sure.

Vinegar: Vinegar is made from wine, beer hops, fruits, grains, sap or honey. It is used in Asian food as a preservative and for its flavoring qualities. White, black, red, rice and sweet vinegars are the most common and they are vastly different from one another. Try to use the specific vinegar called for in the recipes or the result will be quite different from what was intended.

LIST OF RECIPES FOR VEGANS AND OVO-LACTO vegetarians

(V = vegan and O/L = recipe includes either egg or dairy or both)

HOT AND SOUR SALAD

index

Guide to weights and measures

The conversions given in the recipes in this book are approximate. Whichever system you use, remember to follow it consistently, thereby ensuring that the proportions are consistent throughout a recipe.

WEIGHTS

Imperial	Metric
⅓ oz	10 g
½ oz	15 g
¾ oz	20 g
1 oz	30 g
2 oz	60 g
3 oz	90 g
4 oz (¼ lb)	125 g
5 oz (⅓ lb)	150 g
6 oz	180 g
7 oz	220 g
8 oz (½ lb)	250 g
9 oz	280 g
10 oz	300 g
11 oz	330 g
12 oz (¾ lb)	375 g
16 oz (1 lb)	500 g
2 lb	1 kg
3 lb	1.5 kg
4 lb	2 kg

VOLUME

Imperial	Metric	Cup
1 fl oz	30 ml	
2 fl oz	60 ml	¼
3 fl oz	90 ml	⅓
4 fl oz	125 ml	½
5 fl oz	150 ml	⅔
6 fl oz	180 ml	¾
8 fl oz	250 ml	1
10 fl oz	300 ml	1¼
12 fl oz	375 ml	1½
13 fl oz	400 ml	1⅔
14 fl oz	440 ml	1¾
16 fl oz	500 ml	2
24 fl oz	750 ml	3
32 fl oz	1L	4

USEFUL CONVERSIONS

¼ teaspoon	1.25 ml
½ teaspoon	2.5 ml
1 teaspoon	5 ml
1 Australian tablespoon	20 ml (4 teaspoons)
1 UK/US tablespoon	15 ml (3 teaspoons)

Butter/Shortening

1 tablespoon	½ oz	15 g
1½ tablespoons	¾ oz	20 g
2 tablespoons	1 oz	30 g
3 tablespoons	1 ½ oz	45 g

OVEN TEMPERATURE GUIDE

The Celsius (°C) and Fahrenheit (°F) temperatures in this chart apply to most electric ovens. Decrease by 25°F or 10°C for a gas oven or refer to the manufacturer's temperature guide. For temperatures below 325°F (160°C), do not decrease the given temperature.

Oven description	°C	°F	Gas Mark
Cool	110	225	¼
	130	250	½
Very slow	140	275	1
	150	300	2
Slow	170	325	3
Moderate	180	350	4
	190	375	5
Moderately Hot	200	400	6
Fairly Hot	220	425	7
Hot	230	450	8
Very Hot	240	475	9
Extremely Hot	250	500	10

First published in the United States in 2002 by Periplus Editions (HK) Ltd., with editorial offices at 153 Milk Street, Boston, Massachusetts 02109 and 130 Joo Seng Road #06-01/03 Olivine Building Singapore 368357

Commissioned by Deborah Nixon; Text: Vicki Liley; Photographer: Ben Dearnley; Stylist: Vicki Liley; Design Concepts: Kerry Klinner; Editor: Carolyn Miller; Production Manager: Sally Stokes; Project Co-ordinator: Alexandra Nahlous

Printed in India